FRANKLIN PARK PUBLIC LIBRARY

3 1316 00421 9195

W9-ARY-889

WITHDRAWN

FRANKLIN PARK PUBLIC LIBRARY
FRANKLIN PARK, ILL.

Each borrower is held responsible for all library
material drawn on his card and for fines accruing on
the same. No material will be issued until such fine
has been paid.

All injuries to library material beyond reasonable
wear and all losses shall be made good to the
satisfaction of the Librarian.

MAKING CONTACT!

MARCONI GOES WIRELESS

Monica Kulling   *Illustrated by Richard Rudnicki*

FRANKLIN PARK LIBRARY
WITHDRAWN
FRANKLIN PARK, IL

TUNDRA BOOKS

For my brother Edwin,
remembering our radio days
M.K.

J-B
MARCONI
421-9195

For my brother Stephen,
the electrical engineer in the family
R.R.

Special thanks to Henry M. Bradford of Wolfville, Nova Scotia, historian on wireless telegraphy, for generously reading the manuscript, and to Richard Rudnicki for introducing me to Henry. – M.K.

Thanks to Henry M. Bradford for technical support and to Monica Kulling for help with research. Thanks to all my models: Wesley Rimmington, Bob Johnston, Scott Riker, Anthony Kuhn, Darielle Rudnicki, Andrea, Alexander, and Erica Hilchie Pye, Tim Tracey, Charlie Bourne, John Fraser, Matt Andrea, Kyle Jackson, Kevin Robins, and James and Diana Hazelton. And a special thanks to Susan Tooke. – R.R.

Text copyright © 2013 by Monica Kulling
Illustrations copyright © 2013 by Richard Rudnicki

Published in Canada by Tundra Books, a division of Random House of Canada Limited,
One Toronto Street, Suite 300, Toronto, Ontario M5C 2V6

Published in the United States by Tundra Books of Northern New York, P.O. Box 1030, Plattsburgh, New York 12901

Library of Congress Control Number: 2012947610

All rights reserved. The use of any part of this publication reproduced, transmitted in any form or by any means, electronic, mechanical, photocopying, recording, or otherwise, or stored in a retrieval system, without the prior written consent of the publisher – or, in case of photocopying or other reprographic copying, a licence from the Canadian Copyright Licensing Agency – is an infringement of the copyright law.

Library and Archives Canada Cataloguing in Publication

Kulling, Monica, 1952-
        Making contact! : Marconi goes wireless / Monica Kulling ; illustrated by Richard Rudnicki.

(Great idea series)
ISBN 978-1-77049-378-0. – ISBN 978-1-77049-379-7 (EPUB)

        1. Marconi, Guglielmo, marchese, 1874-1937 – Juvenile literature.
2. Inventors – Italy – Biography – Juvenile literature. 3. Radio – History – Juvenile literature. 4. Telegraph, Wireless – Marconi system – History – Juvenile literature. I. Rudnicki, Richard II. Title. III. Series: Great idea series

TK5739M37K85 2013   j621.384092   C2012-905820-3

We acknowledge the financial support of the Government of Canada through the Canada Book Fund and that of the Government of Ontario through the Ontario Media Development Corporation's Ontario Book Initiative. We further acknowledge the support of the Canada Council for the Arts and the Ontario Arts Council for our publishing program.

 **ONTARIO ARTS COUNCIL**
CONSEIL DES ARTS DE L'ONTARIO

Edited by Sue Tate
Designed by Leah Springate
The artwork in this book was rendered in acrylic on 300 lb. hot press watercolor paper.

www.tundrabooks.com

Printed and bound in China

1 2 3 4 5 6   18 17 16 15 14 13

Sources of Inspiration:

Sonneborn, Liz. *Great Life Stories: Guglielmo Marconi: Inventor of Wireless Technology.* New York: Franklin Watts, 2005.

Weightman, Gavin. *Signor Marconi's Magic Box.* London: HarperCollins Publishers, 2003.

Zannos, Susan. *Guglielmo Marconi and the Story of Radio Waves.* Delaware: Mitchell Lane Publishers, 2005.

Internet: www.factmonster.com/biography/var/guglielmomarconi.html

Radio Days

There was a time
all round the world
when Radio was queen.
She waited grandly
in the room
for her subjects
to gather at her feet.
"Give me your ears.
Listen," she said.

So we sat quietly,
hearing stories
that took us to other worlds;
listening to the sounds
of horses' hooves,
block hitting block –
Clip-clop. Clip-clop.

We did nothing but listen.
Imagine.

The storm pelted Benjamin Franklin as he flew his kite on the hill. A lightning bolt struck the wet string and zapped down to the iron key tied at the end. The charge then jolted into a jar designed to store electricity.

As a boy, Guglielmo (*Goo-le-EL-mo*) Marconi loved science and invention. His hero was Benjamin Franklin, who'd flown a kite in a storm to prove that lightning is a charge of electricity.

"There is energy in the air!" announced Marconi excitedly.

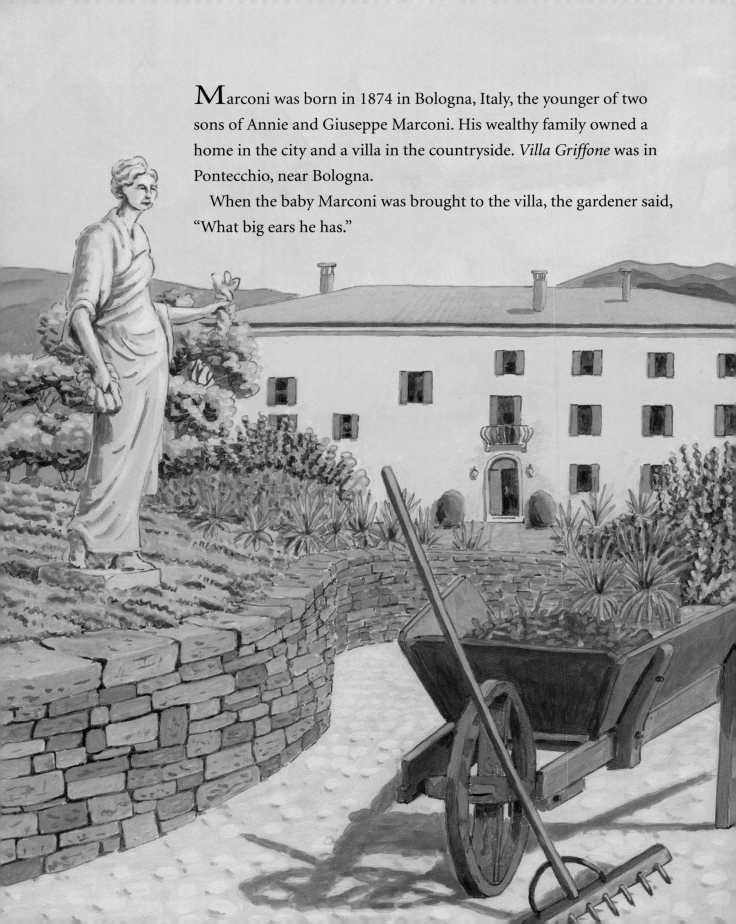

Marconi was born in 1874 in Bologna, Italy, the younger of two sons of Annie and Giuseppe Marconi. His wealthy family owned a home in the city and a villa in the countryside. *Villa Griffone* was in Pontecchio, near Bologna.

When the baby Marconi was brought to the villa, the gardener said, "What big ears he has."

"He will be able to hear the still, small voices in the air," replied Signora Marconi proudly.

These words held a seed of truth, for Guglielmo Marconi would grow up to become the father of wireless communication.

Marconi did not do well in school, so his family hired tutors. By age ten, he was reading the books in his father's library.

The German scientist Heinrich Hertz wrote about radio waves. He produced them by using a high-voltage electric spark. Marconi was fascinated. He learned Morse code, the language of the telegraph. A retired telegraph operator taught him how to tap messages on the telegraph machine.

In 1894, when Marconi was twenty, he and his brother, Alfonso, went on vacation to the Alps, in northern Italy. One night, while trying to fall asleep, Marconi was struck by the spark of a great idea. Could *he* find a way to use radio waves to send wireless messages?

It had never been done before. Marconi would have to act fast if he wanted to be the first.

Marconi was a born inventor. He could concentrate for hours, and, when an experiment failed, he simply started over. But an inventor needed equipment and a place to work.

"We will clear out two attic rooms at *Villa Griffone*," said his mother. She was almost as excited as her son.

"Inventing is a fine hobby," said his father. "But how will you make a living?"

Despite his doubts, Marconi's father gave him money to buy equipment.

Marconi experimented with batteries, antennas, and an electric spark generator. He would be successful if he could send a radio wave signal to the receiver on the other side of the room.

Then one day, in the late summer of 1895, Marconi tapped the telegraph key and the bell on the receiver rang.

"It works!" he told his mother. "The signal is going through the air without wires!"

It was time to test the wireless telegraph over a longer distance. Alfonso and two assistants carried the antennas and receiving equipment more than a mile from the villa over a hill. They brought along a hunting rifle. If the signal from the telegraph came through, they would fire a single shot.

Marconi sat at a table under a tree with the wireless transmitter. He pressed the key three times. Then he waited.

Marconi was certain that radio waves could travel great distances. Mountains or the curve of the earth would not stand in their way. This was the final test of his idea.

Suddenly a gunshot rang out. The signal had been received!

At the age of twenty-one, Marconi had invented a working wireless telegraph.

His Irish mother, Annie, had many relatives in England. In 1896, Annie and Marconi traveled there to show off his invention. When they arrived in London, Annie's nephew Henry Jameson-Davis met them at the train station.

"You need a patent," he told Marconi straight off.

So Marconi filed a patent to protect his wireless telegraph from being copied.

In England, Marconi gave many astonishing demonstrations of his wireless telegraph. One of the most exciting involved Queen Victoria.

The queen's son Albert was recovering from a knee injury on the royal yacht, several miles out to sea. She asked Marconi to set up a wireless telegraph, both at her summer home and on the yacht, so that she could get daily updates on her son's recovery. No one had ever before sent messages from land to a ship at sea or from a ship to land.

Soon Marconi was sending telegrams from the yacht to the summerhouse. Queen Victoria marveled at this new invention.

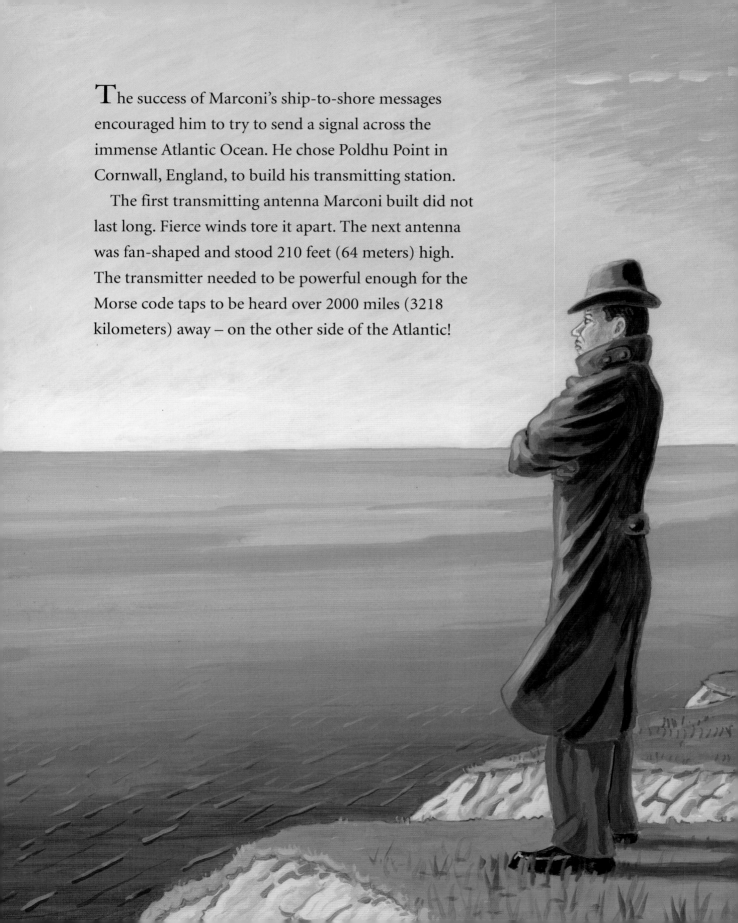

The success of Marconi's ship-to-shore messages encouraged him to try to send a signal across the immense Atlantic Ocean. He chose Poldhu Point in Cornwall, England, to build his transmitting station.

The first transmitting antenna Marconi built did not last long. Fierce winds tore it apart. The next antenna was fan-shaped and stood 210 feet (64 meters) high. The transmitter needed to be powerful enough for the Morse code taps to be heard over 2000 miles (3218 kilometers) away – on the other side of the Atlantic!

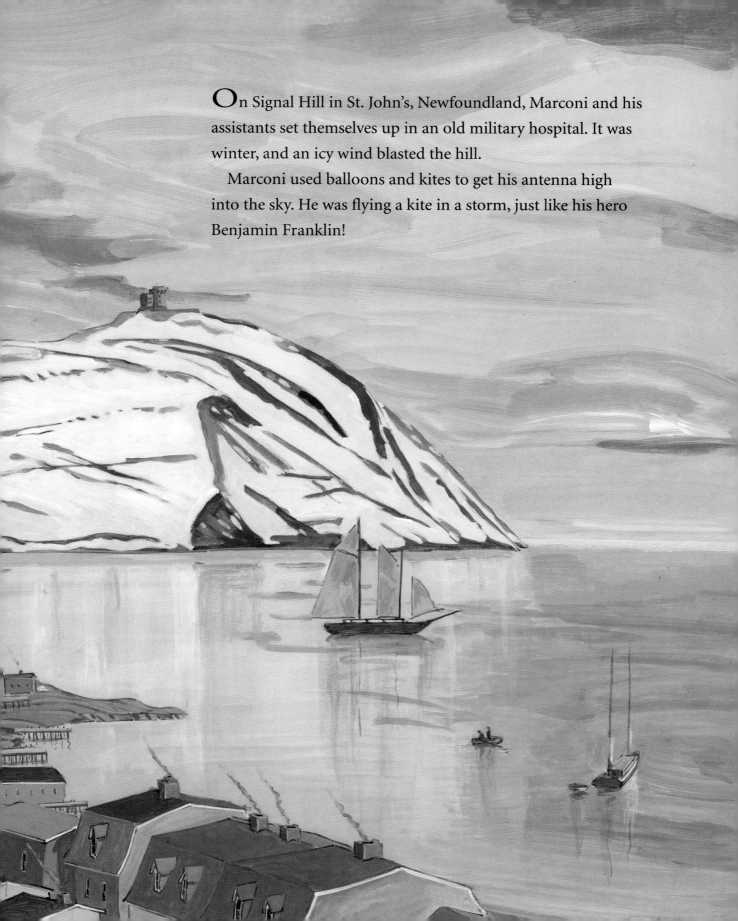

On Signal Hill in St. John's, Newfoundland, Marconi and his assistants set themselves up in an old military hospital. It was winter, and an icy wind blasted the hill.

Marconi used balloons and kites to get his antenna high into the sky. He was flying a kite in a storm, just like his hero Benjamin Franklin!

The Poldhu Point crew sent the Morse code signal for the letter *S* for three hours every day. Marconi listened patiently for the signal through an earpiece, but heard nothing. As the days went by, he grew more and more discouraged.

Finally, on December 12, 1901, Marconi heard three clicks on the receiver. Excitedly, he handed the earpiece to an assistant, who also heard three clicks. The signal was scratchy and faint, but Marconi and his assistant could hear it. Marconi had made contact!

For the first time ever, a wireless signal had traveled the distance between two continents. It was only the beginning.

Save Our Ship!

Over one hundred years ago, the "unsinkable" *Titanic* hit an iceberg and sank on April 15, 1912. There were only 705 survivors out of more than 2200 passengers and crew.

Marconi's wireless telegraph was both a blessing and a curse on that voyage. The *Titanic* received six ice warnings on the day of the collision, but these were ignored. The passengers had been tying up the telegraph with greetings from the middle of the ocean.

The last telegraph sent from the *Titanic* stated: "We are sinking fast, passengers being put into boats."

If not for Marconi's invention, the ship named the *Carpathia* would not have heard the call for help or been able to race to the rescue and locate the survivors. No one would have lived to tell the story.